FILES

0041290305

SCIENCE FILES – WOOD
was produced by

David West 👥 **Children's Books**
7 Princeton Court
55 Felsham Road
London SW15 1AZ

Designers: Rob Shone, Fiona Thorne, David West
Editor: James Pickering
Picture Research: Carrie Haines

First published in Great Britain in 2001 by
Heinemann Library, Halley Court, Jordan Hill,
Oxford OX2 8EJ, a division of Reed Educational and
Professional Publishing Limited.

OXFORD MELBOURNE AUCKLAND
JOHANNESBURG BLANTYRE GABORONE
IBADAN PORTSMOUTH (NH) USA CHICAGO

05 04 03 02 01
10 9 8 7 6 5 4 3 2 1

ISBN 0 431 14300 5 (HB)
ISBN 0 431 14306 4 (PB)

British Library Cataloguing in Publication Data

Parker, Steve, 1952 -
  Wood. - (Science files)
  1. Wood
  I. Title
  620.1'2

Printed and bound in Spain by Bookprint, S.L., Barcelona

PHOTO CREDITS :
Abbreviations: t-top, m-middle, b-bottom, r-right,
l-left.

Front cover - tl - Robert Harding Picture Library. 4tl,
5tr, 6, 6/7, 8bl, 9br, 10bl, 10mr, 11tr, 12t, 12m, 13br,
16br, 16/17t, 17tr, 19tl, 19mr, 24bl, 24/25b, 25m &
br, 26/27, 28bl & tr - Robert Harding Picture Library.
7r (Christian Jegou/Publiphoto Diffusion), 17mr -
Science Photo Library, London. 8m (Jean-Paul
Ferrere), 24/25t (Peter Steyn) - Ardea. 13t - The Rural
History Centre, University of Reading. 14 - AKG
Photo. 14/15 - ISOKON, PLUS, London. 18bl (Eileen
Tweedy/British Museum), 26t (British Museum) - The
Art Archive. 18tr - Sotheby's Picture Library. 21bl -
Bridge of Weir Leather Company Ltd, Scotland. 21br
- Popperfoto. 22t - Mary Evans Picture Library. 23m -
Courtalds.

Every effort has been made to trace the copyright
holders and we apologise in advance for any
unintentional omissions. We would be pleased to
insert the appropriate acknowledgement in any
subsequent edition of this publication.

*An explanation of difficult words can be
found in the glossary on page 30.*

SCIENCE FILES

WOOD

Steve Parker

Heinemann
LIBRARY

CONTENTS

When a tree is cut into logs, you can see circles or rings, one inside the other. These were formed as the tree grew, one circle each year. How old was this tree?

INTRODUCTION

Few materials are as widely available, useful, beautiful and adaptable as wood. We use it to make countless objects, from matchsticks to boats and buildings. We burn wood for light and warmth, and for heat to cook. We create wonderful wooden carvings, statues and other works of art. We also alter or process wood to make paper, card, rayon, resins and many other materials and chemicals. A world without wood would be very different – and not only for us. The lives of millions of animals depend on trees and wood.

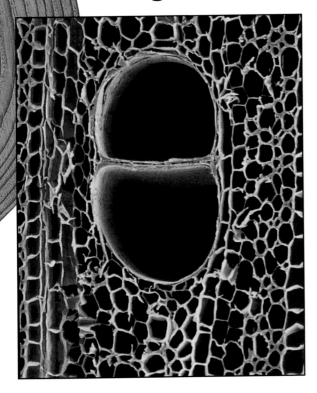

Wood is made of millions of the tiny fibres and tubes of two main substances, cellulose and lignin, with air spaces between them. This is why wood is light yet strong.

Houses, huts, sheds and many other structures are made from wood. Properly cared for, with paints and preservatives, they last for generations.

Wood is mashed up, and has chemicals added to it, to make a thick 'soup' called wood pulp. This is pressed and rolled into sheets. It dries as paper.

WORLD OF WOOD

Woodlands and forests of various kinds cover about one-fifth of the Earth's land surface. The trees in them vary greatly, and each type has its special features and uses.

SOFTWOODS

Softwoods are trees with small, hard, thin, often needle-shaped leaves. They include pines, firs, spruces and cedars. Most of these trees keep their leaves all year round, so they are also known as evergreens. Also, most grow their seeds in hard, woody cones, and so are called coniferous trees (conifers).

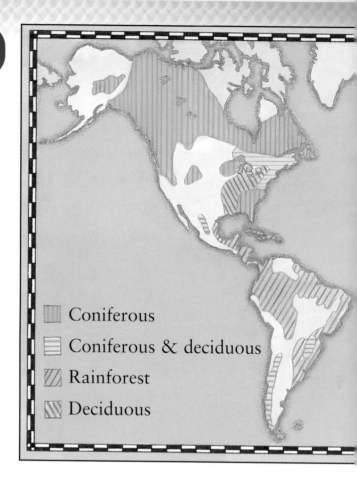

	Coniferous
	Coniferous & deciduous
	Rainforest
	Deciduous

Rainforests thrive where it is wet all year (below). Those in warm places, around the middle of the world, are tropical rainforests. They have more wildlife than anywhere else on Earth.

Forests take years to grow, but hours to destroy.

THE WORLD'S FORESTS

The main conifer, or softwood, forests are in northern lands. Here, the winters are long, cold and snowy. Deciduous woodlands and rainforests of various types usually contain a mixture of hardwood trees.

HARDWOODS

Most hardwood trees are strong and tough. They have wide, flat leaves, and are called broadleaved trees. They include such trees as oak, beech, elm and hickory. In some tropical places, they have leaves all year, so they are evergreen. But usually, old leaves fall in autumn, and new ones grow next spring. These hardwoods are known as deciduous trees.

Facts from the PAST

Millions of years ago, there were no trees like the ones there are today. But there were huge plants, such as ferns, clubmosses and horsetails. The weather was warm and wet, and these plants grew in vast swamps. After they died, their remains were squashed and preserved, and they changed into the type of rock we call coal.

Swamps 300 million years ago.

GROWING FORESTS

Around the world, millions of trees are cut down – every day. New trees take many years to grow. So that we do not run out of wood, we must plant millions more trees – every day.

FOREST FARMS

Farmers grow many crops, like wheat, beans and potatoes. Trees are similar, except that they are bigger and take years to grow. They begin as seeds, taken from the parent tree. The science and methods of growing trees are called forestry.

In the greenhouse, thousands of seeds begin to grow into baby trees – these are called seedlings.

Seedlings grow into young trees, called saplings. These are planted as a forest.

Each of these young trees has a plastic protector. It keeps off frost and also animals such as deer and rabbits, which might nibble and damage it.

HOW FAST DO TREES GROW?

Most softwood trees, such as pines and firs, grow faster than hardwood trees. After 20 years, a Scot's pine reaches 11 metres tall, but an oak is only 9 metres high. The Scot's pine is fully grown and ready to cut down at 60 years old. The oak is still growing at 100 years of age.

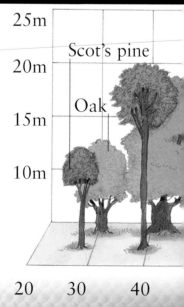

25m

20m

15m

10m

Scot's pine

Oak

20   30   40

MANY TREES THE SAME

Some trees, especially softwoods, are planted in vast forests where there is just one kind of tree. They grow fast, and are all very similar in size and shape. They are known as monoculture stands, and they produce lots of wood. But they are not very rich in wildlife.

LOTS OF DIFFERENT TREES

Other trees, especially hardwoods, grow in more natural woodlands, with many different kinds mixed together. The trees are cut at different times, when each one is ready. This produces less wood, but creates homes for numerous wild animals.

Ideas for the FUTURE

Scientists are changing the genes (growing instructions) in farm plants such as soya, maize and tomatoes. These GM (genetically modified) versions are designed to grow bigger and faster. In the future, perhaps trees will have their genes changed. They will grow faster, stay healthier, and produce better wood.

A scientist altering genes.

A monoculture stand of softwood trees, ready to be harvested. Once they are cut down, new trees will be planted in their place.

60   70   80   90   100 years

When trees are ready to be cut down, or felled, the fellers move in with their chainsaws and huge machines. In a few days, a whole forest can be cleared.

PATTERNS OF FELLING

In selection cutting, only trees of the required size are felled. A few are cut down each year. In clear cutting, all the trees are chopped down and the area is replanted. In seed tree cutting, a few trees are left, to make the seeds that are planted naturally.

Facts from the PAST

For thousands of years, large animals have pulled and lifted massive logs from forests. In South Asia, trained elephants are still used for these tasks. They cause less damage to soil and plant life than huge, heavy vehicles.

Asian elephants and mahouts *(drivers).*

Bark-stripping machines rip off the bark and small side branches. The pieces fall and rot back into the soil, helping future trees to grow.

AXES AND SAWS

Some trees are chopped down with axes or sawn by hand. But most are cut with chainsaws. The feller makes a sideways V-shaped cut in the trunk, so that the tree falls in a certain direction. This causes least damage to the tree itself and its neighbours.

Some trees and bushes are more useful when left alive. Lines of young trees with bendy wood, such as willows or hazels, are woven into 'living fences'.

HEAVY LOADS

Logs of tree trunks and thick branches weigh many tonnes each. Large cranes and powerful trucks are needed to take them out of the forest, to the sawmills, papermills and other places where they will be processed.

Logs may be floated away from the forest as huge rafts (above). However, most logs are hauled by diesel trucks, as long, heavy loads (right).

Trees are living things, and each one grows slightly differently. So when logs arrive at the sawmill, they must be weighed, measured for size and shape, and examined for the quality of the wood and signs of disease.

At a modern sawmill, logs move along tracks, past the whirling saw blades. The people operating the machines stay well clear.

CHECKING THE QUALITY

Logs from mixed forests are from many different types, shapes and sizes of trees. As they arrive at the sawmill, lumber experts mark them with coloured paints, to show the type of wood, and how the log should be sawn. Each sawing pattern produces different sizes and shapes of planks, strips and blocks (right). Some logs have too many hard, dark, dense areas, called knots, where branches grew from the original trunk. These spoil the strength and straightness of the wood. But they can look attractive, and so they may be saved for decorative woodwork.

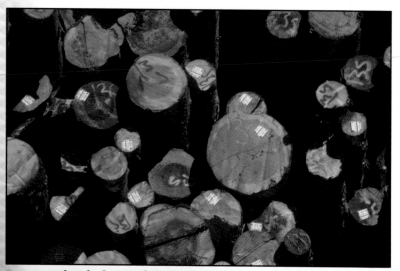

Logs which have been marked, ready for sawing.

Trees grow fast in summer, producing light wood. They almost stop in winter, making a narrow dark band. The results are called growth rings.

WET WOOD

Fresh or 'green' wood, from a recently felled tree, has large amounts of water, sap and natural juices inside it. If this wood is used straight away, it may warp (bend), crack and split as it dries. So first the wood must be carefully dried, or seasoned.

SEASONED WOOD

To season wood naturally, whole or part-sawn logs are left in huge sheds with plenty of fresh air. Drying may take months, even years. To dry it more quickly, it can be put into giant ovens, called kilns, to dry in a few hours.

Through and through

Radial quarter-sawn

Plain-sawn

Block quarter-sawn

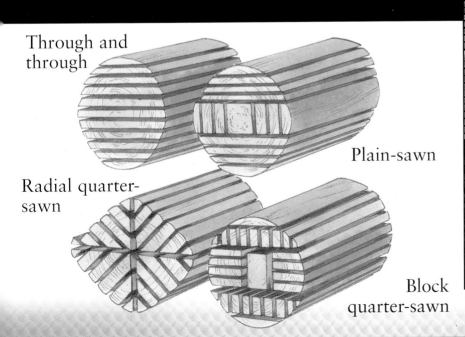

Timber stacked for seasoning.

13

MAKING NEW WOOD

Very few trees grow big enough to be sawn into large, flat sheets, for walls, tables or worktops. So smaller sheets or layers of wood are joined or glued to make larger ones.

THE GRAIN OF WOOD

A piece of wood usually bends more easily in one direction than the other. This follows the wood's grain – the way the tiny fibres form lines. Joining grains in different directions gives better strength.

Facts from the PAST

Paper is made of tiny fibres from wood. Soak paper in water, and its fibres swell and loosen. Then squash and press the wet paper into a shape, add flour as a glue, and it will keep this shape as it dries hard. This material is *papier mâché*. In the past, stage actors often wore painted *papier mâché* masks.

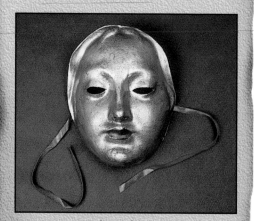

Papier mâché *theatre mask.*

TYPES OF WOODEN BOARDS

PLYWOOD
Flat pieces of wood, called plies, are glued together, with the grains of neighbouring sheets at right angles to each other. This gives strength in both directions. Three-ply has three sheets, and so on.

BLOCKBOARD
This is a 'sandwich' of long strips, or blocks, bonded or glued between two flat sheets. Like plywood, the sheet grains are at right angles to the block grains, for two-way strength.

PARTICLE BOARDS
Chipboards, fibreboards, hardboards and similar sheets are made from small pieces of wood, pressed hard together and glued or bonded by adhesives and resins.

This furniture (left) is all made from plywood. Plywood is made in many different thicknesses. If plies (layers) are heated and dampened by steam, they can be bent around curved surfaces before they are glued (far left).

VENEERS

Veneers are thin sheets or 'leaves' of wood, carefully cut from a log, a bit like peeling an orange. They show wood's grain and other patterns. An item made of ordinary cheap wood can be covered with veneer, to make it appear more beautiful and expensive.

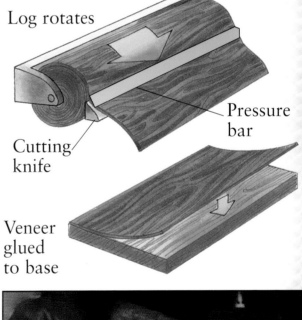

Log rotates

Pressure bar

Cutting knife

Veneer glued to base

MAN-MADE BOARDS

There are hundreds of different kinds of artificial or man-made boards, depending on the way that different layers or pieces are joined together. Chipboard is made from small bits or chips of wood, which come from the sawmill and might otherwise be wasted. Fibreboard is made from wood soaked in chemicals, which split the wood into tiny, hair-like fibres.

INSIDE AND OUT

Most man-made boards are used for making cupboards, furniture, walls, floors and ceilings. Boards used outside must be of good quality, with wood and glues, or adhesives, that are not affected by rain, ice, or the hot, drying sun.

Veneer is carefully glued on.

Cutting, carving, joining and trimming wood are some of the oldest crafts in the world. Each region has its own traditional styles, depending partly on which trees grow there.

Bamboo is not a tree, but a type of giant grass with thick, strong, woody, tube-like stems. These have many uses, such as scaffolding poles.

A house frame has different-sized beams, depending on the weight they support. Board walls are called cladding.

WOODEN BUILDINGS

More than two-thirds of all wood is used for building houses, bridges and similar structures. In areas with plentiful forests, timber is used for almost every part of a house, from the thick beams of the main framework to the flat shingles (tiles) on the roof. The wood is first treated with preservatives, so that it does not rot or go soft, and so that wood-boring insects and other pests do not eat it away. Wood may also be treated with chemicals to slow the spread of flames, since fire is always a hazard.

Joiners use many special tools.

WOODWORKING SKILLS

Carpenters work with most kinds of wood and wooden objects, especially large-scale structures. Joiners usually make smaller items such as furniture and cupboards. Great skill is needed to choose the best type of wood for the job. Items that suffer a lot of wear are usually made from hardwoods such as oak.

JOINING WOOD

There are dozens of ways of joining wood, from simply using glue or hammering in nails, to carving complex shapes such as wedge-like dovetails. Each type of joint has its own special strengths. Joints do not only hold pieces of wood together. They show the cabinet-maker's skills and make a wooden item much more valuable.

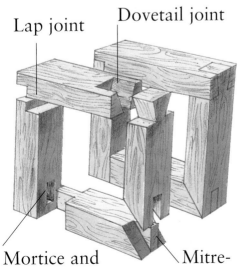

Lap joint

Dovetail joint

Mortice and tenon joint

Mitre-tongue joint

Even hi-tech concrete relies on wood. The concrete is poured into a mould made from wooden shutters (boards), which are later removed.

No two pieces of wood are the same. The colours, patterns, lines of grain and swirling knots are always slightly different. This means every wooden item, from a spoon to a huge table, is unique. Some of the world's most valuable objects are pieces of furniture, made by skilled craftspeople long ago.

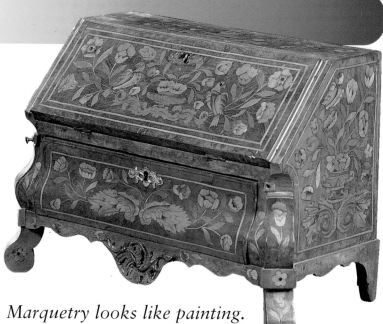

Marquetry looks like painting. But it is done with thin shapes of various kinds of wood. The design is assembled like a jigsaw.

Facts from the PAST

Some of the greatest works of art are wooden statues and carvings, and pictures, scenes and designs cut into sheets of wood, known as woodcuts. One of the most famous artists in wood was Albrecht Dürer, a German painter and engraver (1471–1528).

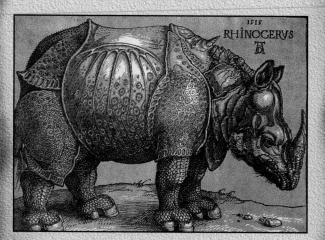

Woodcut by Albrecht Dürer.

MARQUETRY

Marquetry is making pictures from wood. Veneers of different wood types are carefully cut into shapes. They are fixed or applied to a base to create pictures and patterns.

MAKING WOODCUT PRINTS

Before modern printing, many copies of pictures and words could be made using woodcuts. First, the design is marked out.

Next, part of the design is cut away using mallets, chisels and gouges. This leaves a raised design on the wood.

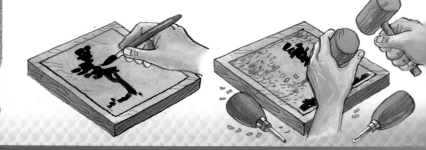

FINISHING WOOD

Wood that is bare or untreated gathers dust and dirt, and may get marked with unsightly smears. So most wooden objects are treated, or finished, with a range of substances. Polishes make wood smooth and shiny, and 'bring out' the grain and colours, making them stronger. Varnishes and lacquers are similar, and also protect the wood from many chemicals, stains, and the effects of wear and tear.

Wood's colour can be changed with purpose-made stains or dyes. These soak into the wood and alter its appearance, but still let the grain patterns show through.

An ink-soaked roller is passed over the surface of the woodcut. The ink stays on the higher areas of the wood.

A sheet of paper is laid on the woodcut and pressed with a clean roller. The ink on the higher parts of the wood sticks to it.

The paper is peeled off to reveal the design in ink. Always remember, it's back to front!

Some Native American people carve 'totem poles' – tree trunks with shapes of animals, plants and spirits.

19

Artists' materials such as charcoal sticks and turpentine are made from wood.

Not all trees that are cut down are used as whole wood. About one in every ten is altered, or processed, using heat, pressure, powerful acids and solvents, and similar substances. The result is a wide range of chemicals and other products obtained from wood.

'DESTROYING' WOOD

To get chemicals from wood, the wood is shredded, heated, and attacked by solvents, under great pressure. The wood breaks down or dissolves into a mushy soup. This is heated again in tall towers called columns.

At each stage, chemicals from the original wood are given off, or evaporated, as gases, and then turned back into liquids in collecting tanks. Burning waste wood provides heat for the whole process.

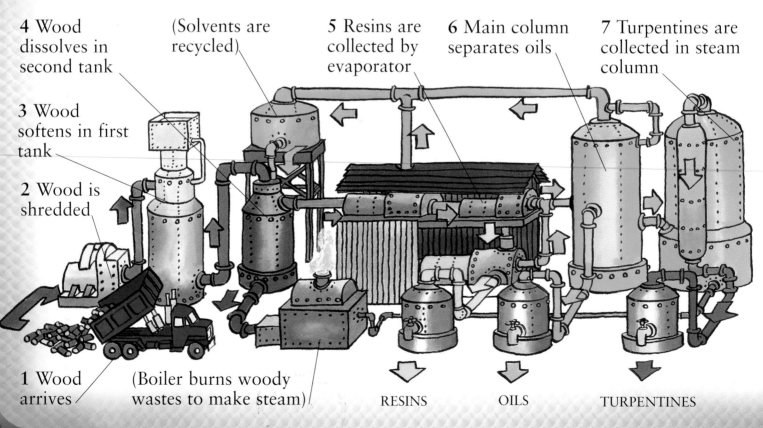

4 Wood dissolves in second tank

(Solvents are recycled)

5 Resins are collected by evaporator

6 Main column separates oils

7 Turpentines are collected in steam column

3 Wood softens in first tank

2 Wood is shredded

1 Wood arrives

(Boiler burns woody wastes to make steam)

RESINS   OILS   TURPENTINES

USEFUL WOOD CHEMICALS

The chemicals made from wood have many uses. Resins and pitches are used to preserve wooden objects like boats, fences and sheds, and as glues. Wood oils are used to make waterproofing substances, soaps, inks and glues. Turpentines are used as paint thinners, as cleaners, and to dissolve other chemicals.

Gymnasts use a resin powder made from wood, rosin, to give a good grip. Rosin is also used on violin bows.

MORE WOODY CHEMICALS

About half of wood's weight is the substance cellulose. This is broken down by strong chemicals such as acids and enzymes, to make sugars. The sugars can be made into molasses syrup, to feed cattle. Or yeast is added to them to convert, or ferment, them into a type of alcohol, called ethanol. This is used as fuel in some cars, or it can be used as a solvent.

Animal skins are made into leather by tanning. Some chemicals for tanning come from tree bark, especially black wattle tree bark.

Facts from the PAST

Before the development of the modern chemical industry, people obtained many of the substances they needed for daily life from nature – especially trees. In Ancient Egypt, dead bodies were preserved as mummies, using chemicals obtained by heating wood.

Ancient Egyptian mummy.

21

Wood can be made into clothes, scarves and other textile items! The substance cellulose, which makes up about half of wood's weight, is the basis for the artificial fibre, rayon.

A NEW INVENTION

Most fibres are natural, like cotton from cotton plants, or wool from sheep. Rayon was the first artificial (man-made) fibre to be invented, in the 1880s. At first it was called artificial silk. In the 1920s its name was changed to rayon and it was very popular.

Clothes made from rayon are soft and supple, but also strong and long-lasting.

MAKING RAYON

Rayon is an artificial fibre, but it has natural origins. Wood chips and bits of waste are pulped into a soup with solvents and other chemicals. Cellulose forms a separate layer in the pulp, and is poured or skimmed off.

Cellulose sheets are the main raw material for rayon. The cellulose is heated with caustic soda. It breaks into flakes, which are then added to another chemical, called carbon disulphide.

Viscose is aged and cleaned

Sheets of cellulose are soaked in caustic soda

Sheets are broken into flakes

Flakes are mixed with carbon disulphide

Caustic soda is mixed in to make viscose

USES OF RAYON

Today, rayon is less popular, since there are many other artificial fibres. But it is fairly cheap and easy to make, so it is still produced in regions with plenty of spare wood. Rayon also has other uses. It forms the rope-like strengthening cords inside vehicle tyres. And it soaks up, or absorbs, liquids well, so is used for medical pads and dressings.

Viscose ready to be forced through spinnerets to make rayon.

Ideas for the FUTURE

Rayon was popular until the 1940s. Then a new artificial fibre, nylon, took over many of its uses. However, nylon is made partly from chemicals in crude oil (petroleum). In the future, crude oil may run out. People might go back to growing trees, to make more rayon again.

Nylon may run out one day.

The mixture, viscose, is left for a few days to 'age'. After cleaning to remove wastes and air bubbles, the viscose is squirted through tiny holes, spinnerets, into liquid sulphuric acid. It turns into flexible strands – rayon.

Rayon filaments (strands) emerging from spinnerets.

Pump

Viscose is vacuum treated to remove air bubbles

Viscose is forced through spinneret into bath of sulphuric acid

The rayon yarn is wound on spools

Charcoal kilns, Malawi.

In addition to wood and chemicals, trees provide many other products. Some are collected from trees growing in forests. Others are obtained from the wood or other parts of the tree, using complicated methods.

Extracts of ginkgo (maidenhair tree) are in this gel. The shampoo contains oil from palm trees.

RUBBER

All rubber originally came from trees. Now there are many different kinds of artificial or man-made rubber. But natural rubber is still used to make certain things, such as aircraft tyres.

Natural rubber is soft, bendy and elastic. It comes from trees such as the hevea (rubber tree). A small cut is made in the tree's bark. Milky liquid sap, called latex, seeps into a small cup fixed to the tree. This is called rubber tapping. Latex is mostly water, with about one-third rubber. It is added to acid chemicals and dried to make pure rubber.

OILS AND EXTRACTS

For thousands of years, people have used natural oils from trees. These are often based on sap, a liquid which is like the tree's 'blood', carrying minerals and nutrients around inside it. Or they are taken, or extracted, from a tree's leaves, fruits, seeds or nuts. Some oils and extracts are used as medicines. They are put into ointments, pills or vapours. Others are used simply because they have a pleasing smell!

Not all woods are used for their strength. The cork tree has soft, light wood with many air spaces in it. It is used to make stoppers for bottles. Balsa is another soft, very light wood.

Natural rubber comes from plantations (forests) of rubber trees (below). Latex is hung out as sheets to dry (inset), and used for softer products such as surgeon's gloves.

Facts from the PAST

Ancient people believed that the hard, shiny, golden substance called amber was made from the rays of the setting sun. In fact, it is sticky, liquid sap or resin which oozed from a cut in a tree's bark, long ago. It set hard, to seal the cut. Lumps of amber are preserved as fossils from prehistoric times. Some contain small animals that got trapped in the stickiness, millions of years ago.

An insect trapped in amber.

The paper that this page is made of was once a tree. About one-tenth of all trees are grown specially to be mashed into a soup-like pulp, by machines and chemicals, and made into paper, card and board. It is a long and complex industrial process, and uses huge amounts of chemicals and energy.

Facts from the PAST

Papyrus from Ancient Egypt.

FROM WOOD ... TO PULP ...

4 Chips are dissolved in boiling chemicals to form wood pulp

2 Bark is stripped and chipped

3 Logs are chipped

Pulp is made from freshly cut logs – and also old paper, card and board, sawmill chips, old rags and clothes, spare straw and reeds, and many other waste or recycled materials.

5 Wood and bark pulps are combined and washed

7 Pulp is stored

1 Logs and other raw materials arrive

6 Pulp is mixed to fine liquid and cleaned

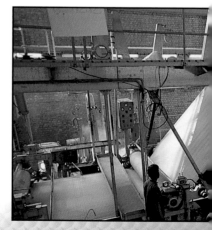

Nearly all paper is made from softwood trees, grown for this purpose. They are much less expensive than hardwood trees, and also their fibres are longer.

FIBRES AND SHEETS

Paper has only been mass-produced from wood in the last 200 years. Before this, fibres of plants such as flax and hemp were used. And before this, writing and pictures were done on parchments (animal skins), or papyrus made from reeds.

The substance called cellulose is in the form of fibres held together by another substance, lignin. When wood is pulped, the lignin is removed or dissolved, so that the fibres become loose and separate. They are then mixed with various liquids and chemicals, and spread out as large layers on rollers. As the layers are pressed thinner and heated, the fibres flatten together and dry. They form sheets of paper, or thicker card, or even thicker board.

... TO PAPER

Pulp is mixed with bleaching chemicals, to make white paper, or with pigment dyes for other colours. The headbox spreads out the pulp as a wide layer on a wire-mesh belt.

The pulp layer is pressed hard to make it much thinner and squash the fibres together. It passes through heated drums, and calender rollers add chemicals, such as a glossy finish.

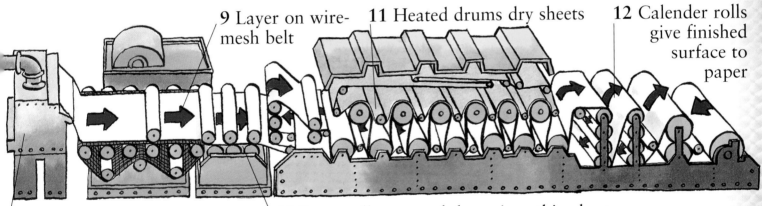

9 Layer on wire-mesh belt

11 Heated drums dry sheets

12 Calender rolls give finished surface to paper

8 Headbox spreads out pulp

10 Press rollers squash layer into thin sheet

Sheets of paper on the press are metres wide and kilometres long (left). They are cut into smaller rolls to take to book printers and other users (right).

Wood will remain a vital material – not only for houses, furniture, paper and other products. The trees grown for wood give food and shelter to animals. They give out the oxygen we need to breathe, and hold soil so that it is not washed or blown away.

Fuelwood for fires is very scarce in many countries. It can take half a day just to collect a few small twigs. If young trees are not planted, the supplies of wood will run out.

PLANT MORE TREES!

In some parts of the world, new trees are planted to replace the trees we cut down. Here, wood is a renewable resource. But in other parts of the world, areas of forest are cut down for timber, then the soil is used for a few years for crops, then as grazing for farm animals, then – nothing. No new trees are planted for future use. The bare soil washes or blows away. This destruction happens especially in the richest forests of all, the tropical rainforests.

As well as planting more trees, we can use the trees and wood we already have, in better ways. Rare hardwood timbers such as teak and mahogany should come from forests which are properly managed, or sustainable. This means new trees are planted as old ones are felled, and also the animals, plants and soil are cared for. We can recycle paper, card and wooden items, and re-use wood itself in many ways.

Bales of used paper ready for recycling.

This symbol is used to show products that are made from recycled materials.

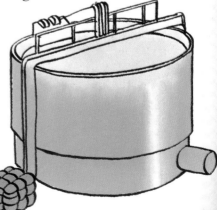

Newspapers, glossy paper (magazines) and card are collected separately and put into the correct paper banks.

Paper for recycling is collected from the banks, pressed into bales, and taken to the papermill.

The bales are put into a hydrapulper vat of chemicals, to make recycled products such as paper towels.

TYPE OF WOOD		FEATURES AND USES
HARDWOODS	Beech	Smooth, hard and strong; used for flooring, furniture, frames
	Elm	Strong, irregular grain; used for furniture, boatbuilding
	Mahogany	Dark and hard; used for carvings, panels, furniture, instruments
	Maple (soft)	Light, straight-grained; used for furniture, joinery, veneers, musical instruments, floorboards, wall panels, plywood
	Oak (European)	Pale but tough; used for furniture, joinery, outside woodwork
	Teak	Uneven grain, oily; used for joinery, outdoor furniture, veneers
	Walnut	Dark with distinctive grain and knots; used for furniture, carving, veneers, joinery, gun stocks (handles)
SOFTWOODS	Cedar (red)	Scented, fairly soft but long-lasting; used for chests, boxes, houses, roofing
	Cypress (Eurasian)	Durable and long-lasting; used for doors, window frames
	Fir (Douglas)	Obtained in large, knot-free sizes; used for buildings, plywood and other boards, cladding, poles, some joinery and furniture
	Hemlock (Western)	Even, straight, prominent grain; used for construction and in buildings, plywood, joinery
	Larch	Straight, pale and tough; used for beams, props, boat planks
	Pine (Parana)	Even and close-grained; very high resin content; used for doors, tables, chairs, cabinets
	Sequoia (redwood)	Varies from fine to stringy; trees can grow to enormous size; used for roofs, cladding
	Spruce (Norway)	Pale and even; used for joinery, floorboards, musical instruments, boxes
	Yew	Hard, long-lasting; used for furniture, joinery, handles, shafts

GLOSSARY

cellulose
A material that makes up about half the weight of wood. It contains small fibres, linked end to end like beads on a necklace.

clear cutting
When all the trees in a stand (patch of forest) are chopped down. The area is usually then replanted.

dissolve
To turn from a solid into a liquid.

grain
The way that the fibres in wood make a pattern of lines.

hardwood
Wood from a tree that usually has broad leaves which fall off in winter. The group includes some of the softest woods, such as cork.

lignin
A material that makes up about one-quarter of the weight of wood. It gives strength to the wood and binds the cellulose fibres together.

rayon
An artificial fibre, derived from wood and used in fabrics and tyres.

resin
A sticky substance in a tree's bark and wood. It protects the tree from pests and seals cuts in the bark.

sap
A liquid of minerals and nutrients that circulates around plants.

seed tree cutting
When most of the trees in a stand (patch of forest) are chopped down, leaving some to produce seeds that grow into new trees.

softwood
Wood from a tree that usually has needle-like leaves all year round, and generally grows its seeds in cones. The group includes some tough woods, like yew and juniper.

solvent
A chemical which is good at dissolving other substances.